Pathways to Unlimited Joy

Joy Ani

Free permission of use of scripture quotations NKJV, NLT, NIV ,KJV

For enquiries, email: info@joyofmanygenerations.com

www.joyofmanygenerations.com

ISBN: 978-0-9931282-2-6

DEDICATION

What shall I say unto the Lord? All I have to say is thank you God the Father, the Son and the Holy Spirit for helping me to turn my lemons to lemonade and enabling me to serve generations with it. I am grateful!

I also want to dedicate this book to the whole world, for thriving through the suffering that the COVID-19 pandemic brought to humanity. My heart goes out to those who lost their loved ones, suffered mental issues, breakdown of marriages, financial losses, to mention a few.

It was also a dark time in my life, watching my loved ones go through pains, depression, etc. However, the joy of the Lord saw me through. This is the main reason behind writing this book - Pathways to Unlimited Joy.

ACKNOWLEDGEMENTS

I would like to thank all the people God has brought my way in fulfilling this vision, most especially my Book Coach, Florence Igboayaka - you are amazing. Thank you for believing in my vision and seeing to it that it became a reality. My prayer for you is that your vision will not die and all your good heart desires shall come to pass in Jesus name. Nkem Memkiti thank you so much for your professionalism in editing this book. You are indeed a Prof!

A huge thank you to Reverend Bola Akintola and Minister Kikelomo Adebiyi, for sharing your stories to encourage others and also for taking out time from your busy schedule to review the manuscript, you are simply the best. May God honour you both in Jesus name.

To Minister Blessing Theophilus-Israel, thank you for taking time to review the manuscript. You are indeed a blessing. You never get tired of taking my calls. My prayer is that each time you call on the Lord, He will answer you speedily in Jesus name.

REVIEWS

If I were to ask you the difference between Joy and happiness, you would probably conclude that they mean the same thing. Whilst both are expressions of emotions, they have different meanings.

Joy Ani, in her book titled "Pathways to Unlimited Joy", has clearly explained what differentiates the two. I was really happy to read the manuscript and I believe this book has been written for such an unprecedented time as this! The whole world is in turmoil and there is so much misery around. No nation has been spared of the pandemic and the pain and sorrow that has come with it. At the time of writing this review, the world is still grasping with and mopping up its effects.

However, in the midst of all these, joy can be found. The book takes us through some pains the author herself went through and stories of other people as well as how they overcame. I particularly enjoyed reading the stories as each one recounted their pain and eventual joy through different lenses.

The beauty of the book is also the fact that it is written from a biblical perspective, which traces true Joy as coming from the Almighty God, the author of life and the one who loves you and me. One thing I personally believe is that Joy is contagious, which means I can spread it wherever I go. I do not need to be miserable neither should you, because God wants us to be happy and experience unlimited joy. While the devil loves to see us miserable and unhappy continuously, our God created us to enjoy life abundantly and to radiate His joy to the fullest.

The bible says in Psalm 30:5 that *"weeping may last through the night, but joy comes with the morning"* (NLT). This scripture is a source of comfort to me and it means that no matter the pain or discomfort I may be going through, it will not last forever, but will surely end on a note of Joy.

I will highly recommend this book to anyone going through challenging times or anyone who wants to be an encouragement to others.

Kikelomo Adebiyi

Co-founder, Rapha Nurturing Academy

REVIEWS

We know that things do not always go as we plan in life, in fact, as the author says, sometimes life gives us lemons. What we choose to do with those lemons is the essence of this book. This book is great at showing us how we can overcome all obstacles and choose to live a life of joy based on Biblical principles. In this unique book, we learn the real meaning of joy, how we can find and have this joy.

We are given nuggets to help us to respond to life trials with joy, which may sound easier said than done but the book practically shows us how. The book shows readers how to accept any situation that arises. The author shares her powerful testimonies of overcoming the storms in her life and how she maintained her joy through it all.

The book also demonstrates the importance of suffering, as it allows us to minister and comfort those who are also suffering. The book outlines important tools on how to obtain unlimited joy including the act of gratitude and importance of counting our blessings.

I would highly recommend this book for those who seek the source of unlimited joy in their lives.

Blessing Theophilus-Israel

Christian Millionaire BookClub®

Joy Ani's book on Pathway to Unlimited Joy is an invaluable tool for unlocking the truths about joy. Joy is a vital ingredient needed on a daily basis, especially during these challenging times, without it we lose our strength - the Bible states that the joy of the Lord is our strength. Joy is therefore a vital necessity.

This book rightly differentiates between happiness (a temporary state) and joy (a permanent state). This book will certainly assist the reader to appropriate joy and live the joy filled life God expects of him or her.

I recommend this book, as it is an easy and enjoyable read. It will refresh the knowledge of some and introduce others to the indispensable element of the Fruit of the Holy Spirit- the Spirit of Joy.

Enjoy as you delve into the nuggets and life changing truths in this book.

Bolanle Akintola (Rev.)

Beulah Ministries International.

TABLE OF CONTENTS

INTRODUCTION

Everyone on the face of the earth has a story to tell of how life has left a bitter taste in their mouth. Life gives lemons to everyone born of a woman, with no exception to the rule. As the common saying goes, "we all have stories to tell", even when we look all put together and radiant on the outside.

After an encounter, you may feel bad, resentful or bitter about life and that should actually be the normal reaction. In fact, when you do not react like that, people might feel that you need to be cross-examined.

However, people have different ways of reacting to such encounters which translates to how joyful they become in the end or otherwise. There are those who go through pains and agonies without looking an inch of what they went through until they tell you, while there are others who epitomise the problems. They can rightly be tagged "problem personified" when looked upon at a first glance. These people are also likely to have never believed that someone can go through life's battles and come out victorious and unscathed.

The former scenario is replete across the globe and in every facet of life. It is no respecter of religion, status, culture, family background, age or gender.

A lot of people genuinely want to be joyful and as such, they look for solutions from places and things that can only give temporary happiness. Sadly, a great number in this category, have destroyed their lives in the course of searching for these solutions through other means or avenues that do not truly have the answers.

Stories are told of how people fall into depression and consequently, drug abuse or getting involved with other immoral practices, all in the course of searching for that joy that should give them inner peace. Some unfortunately, end up dying in the process. This number is increasing daily with only a few percentage finding a permanent solution.

However, the truth is, permanent joy can be achieved because there is indeed a pathway to finding it and experiencing it in this life.

My purpose is to help you partake in the experience of this joy that I already have, so join me as I show you how I turned my lemons to lemonade as I present my life's testimony in this book.

GOAL

When an author embarks on the project of penning down words that should turn into a book, he or she has a mission to impart and impact people's lives. This is my heart's desire and prayer as you read this book.

My ultimate mission is (by the grace of God) to show people across nations and races a better way of living a joyful life based on Biblical principles through this book.

I sincerely pray and trust that as you are already in possession of this book, you will have an encounter that will change your life for good with regards to the understanding of the meaning of God's kind of Joy.

The Holy Bible in the book of Nehemiah 8:10 [KJV] says that *'The Joy of the Lord is my strength'*.

Also in Habakkuk 3:17-18 [KJV], the Word of God states that *'Though the fig tree shall not blossom neither shall the fruit be in the vines, the labour of the olive shall fail and the fields shall yield no meat, the flock shall be cut off from the fold and there shall be no herd in the stalls..., yet will I rejoice in the Lord, I will joy in the God of my salvation'.*

These scriptures clearly affirm and validate the fact that the true source of joy for anyone who sincerely seeks and longs for it, is the Maker and originator Himself, God Almighty. After all, it was He who crafted us and breathed His kind of life into us, so how else do we expect to live or find happiness outside His nature or will?

Someone rightly explains this with a very good analogy. He said that for you to maximize the use of any product you purchase, you must understand what the manufacturer says about the product in the manual. If not, the resultant effect will be guess work which will ultimately end up in abuse and/or destruction of that product.

This is so true with many people, even the so-called believers. Many of us do not want to live within God's terms and conditions which are anchored on The Bible - the errorless and impregnable word of God. We choose to live on our own terms which are basically convenient to us. In the end when it boomerangs and we experience pain, we then want Him to take the responsibility.

God who is forever merciful, comes to our rescue when we ask Him but His whole intention is that we do not allow things get to that level in the first place before seeking His face.

John 15:5 [KJV] says, *'I am the Vine, ye are the branches, he that abideth in me and I in him, the same bringeth much fruit for without me ye can do nothing...'* In other words, there is no real joy if we disconnect from the Source.

Genesis 1:28 [KJV] clearly states God's original plan and intention for man even before the fall of man. It says, *'And God blessed them and God said unto them, be fruitful and multiply and replenish the earth and subdue it and have dominion over the fish of the sea, and over the fowl of the air and over every living thing that moveth upon the earth'*.

Can you see? There was never a time in God's plan that man, (i.e. you and I), were meant to suffer and live without joy. Ours was to come and establish God's kingdom here on earth by taking charge over everything He promised us and making sure that they remain under us while we remain under Him. That is the hierarchy. Unfortunately, man fell by choosing to go his way.

When man fell and sin came into the world, the all-knowing God, had a master plan in Christ Jesus so that as many as receive Him, will not suffer the pain and agony of perpetual sadness or pain caused by sin.

I know that some will struggle to accept this submission as a result of their beliefs. My intention is not to start off an argument but to present the truth to you from a Biblical perspective, as to what joy is all about as well as how to attain and keep it God's way. The Bible remains the one and only manual for all those who profess Christianity.

HIGHLIGHTS:

Pertinent questions likely to be asked are narrowed to these two points:

1. What is the real source of joy?

2. How can one find and have this joy?

From my introduction, you will agree with me that there are people cut across all strata of the society that this book should be a must-read for. This book contains a few of the specifics that one needs to know in order to get out of the bondage that the enemy has kept them in. Real knowledge about anything is just mental exercise but true knowledge of specific subject like Joy, is embedded in God Himself. As it is written in the Holy Bible *'you shall know the truth and the truth shall set you free'*, John 8:32 [KJV].

So, who is this book written for? Who will this book be beneficial to?

1. Christians: there is the possibility that this can be controversial because some with sanctimony and spirituality might want to argue that every Christian, by reason of their salvation ought to

live with joy. Even you reading this book might also be wondering along that line, why should Christians be added to this category? I dare say, why not? It will surprise you to know that a number of Christians too have not gotten to the knowledge of this truth as a result of doctrinal beliefs and dogmas that have been raised above the knowledge God's word thus truncating God's eternal purpose in their lives.

2. Those ignorant of the existence of real joy: It is said that what you do not know cannot kill you, however, it's very unfortunate that what people do not know has actually destroyed many of them and can destroy more if Biblical principles and perspectives are not understood and practiced. The Bible says '*my people perish for lack of knowledge*' Hosea 4:1[KJV].

Can you see that? It is God's people not just the people which means that Christians can also be ignorant in some important things concerning the Kingdom. Therefore we need to find out some truths in order to enjoy to the fullest. As it is written, '*These things I have spoken to you, that my joy might remain in you and that your joy may be full*' John 15:11[KJV]. As we climax the age, the enemy's buffeting will be on the increase and until you are grounded in the Word, it will be difficult to comprehend some trials that may arise as a result of the pressure. This book intends to encourage those of us who have professed Christ Jesus to remain steadfast and unmovable if and when such things come on this life's journey and also to show those outside, the path to this joy.

3. People who are facing life's challenges, associated with mental health, like depression and other emotional issues resulting from various battles which they may have caused by themselves or might not have. Such people can be self-destructive when they become overwhelmed by guilt or delusions of what should improve their self-worth other than the Creator Himself. They need to know that forgiveness that can bring God's type of joy is still possible no matter the cause of the pain becomes paramount and this is the essence of this book - Pathways to unlimited joy.

4. People who are waiting for answers to their age-long prayers. This set of people will need to understand that one can be joyful while waiting

patiently for a miracle and that as a matter of fact, joy is the lubricant that makes the wait easier. In this case, it becomes a virtue that God sees and honours. Job 14:14 (KJV) says *'if a man dies, shall he live again? All the days of my appointed time will I wait till my change come'*. In other words, this set of people will appreciate the cliché that says 'when there is life, there is hope'.

5. People who are about to throw in the towel as a result of frustration, having waited for so long. This category looks similar to the one above but it is not the same. They are ones who even those in the patient category see as motivators because they have gone through long suffering and perseverance. People like these usually seem diligent and flawless in character but are always met with resistance by the enemy at the door of a breakthrough, causing the breakthrough not to culminate. They get ridiculed and even labelled by others as those with the 'near success' syndrome that have defied all interventions including spiritual intervention. I call such people giants. If they understand the spiritual, they will rejoice in

their state. However, if one does not know, one may abort his or her miracle during such tests.

6. Those who never believe that true joy exists on this side of life. These people are tougher to convince when it comes to understanding God's kind of joy. They have internalised pain and taken it as their personal cross. Such people have conceived and even idolised the belief that it is the will of God for them to live in it permanently or, until God decides to change His mind. Most of them see lack of joy caused by the hardship they go through as the measurement for their faith in God Himself. They can be very religious but not spiritual. The Bible describes such people in 2 Peter 3:5 [KJV], *'For this they willingly are ignorant of, that by the word of God the heavens were of old, and the earth standing out of the water and in the water'*. This truth can be established to them as they embrace the true Joy that comes from God.

CHAPTER 1

Understanding Joy

There is no one born of a woman that does not crave for joy, whether temporarily or permanently. This is because, from creation God's intention is that man should constantly radiate His glory and part of that glory is joy. By nature man was also created to relate cordially without prejudice and if that happens, the expression of good emotions should be the results. So, joy is a contagious experience that does not remain only with the owner but can affect those around him/her.

I must begin by establishing this fact that joyfulness is different from happiness, as the latter is often associated with external events.

So, what is joy? According to the Oxford dictionary, joy is a feeling of great pleasure and Happiness. If it is a feeling then there must be a force that causes the feeling.

In my words, I would define joy as a deep state of contentment that is not dependent on what is happening around one. It is a state of mind that is at peace and a heart that is satisfied with what is available in the present despite the lack of one's desires at certain times. Joy comes from the root word meaning 'merry-hearted'.

In the Bible, precisely the New Testament, Jesus made a statement which formed part of his final words on earth before ascending to heaven. He requested The Father on behalf of His disciples, 'that they might have joy'. This also refers to all who would come to believe because of their witness, which of course, includes you and me.

The Greek word for joy (chara) also means 'calm delight'. As believers, we should know that Joy is also part of the fruit of the Holy Spirit. Ultimately, these explanations leave a believer with the surety that joy is a blessing available to every child of God, and the Holy Spirit, is The Source.

Our sense of joy should come from knowing that God has our entire lives in His hand and will always make a way where there seems to be none. Joy is a permanent gift; it stays with you as long as you are a believer.

There is a clear cut difference between the joy and happiness. Since we have explained what joy is, we will then go on to define happiness.

As much as we all know that happiness is a beautiful experience and should be encouraged, we must also realise that happiness is temporary, it comes and goes away after what triggers it subsides or leaves.

Happiness always occurs as a result of external situations. It comes when triggered by another person's action or circumstance and is reactionary most times.

So, If I may ask - if you were given a chance to choose between the two, which will you choose for your life? I know you would go for the joy, won't you? Well, it is not just a possibility, it is actually available for you, as you can enjoy it right now.

From the foundation of the earth, when He made man {you and I}, God's intention is that we should live a joyful life. You have a good reason to be joyful because it is your Father's pleasure to give you the gift of joy. All you need do is to ask for it and you will receive His joy. What a great assurance as the song writer succinctly puts it, 'Blessed assurance'.

1.1 Difference between Joy and happiness

Joy is not like happiness which is based on happenstance. Happiness is always predicated on the occurrence of good circumstances. On the other hand, joy is what you are, your disposition, regardless of what is happening around you. Joy is therefore, that inner peace that characterises you, making you who you are in the midst of lack and or abundance.

Joy is also that beautiful emotion inside you which absorbs the negative vibes that filter in and dissipates it. It is in a nutshell, that expression of the gladness of heart which emanates from the soul, with the knowledge that something good will eventually come out of any negative situation or circumstance you experience. This is nothing short of pure joy.

It is also known as a gift from the Holy Spirit and is one of the fruit of the Spirit. It is natural or human to think that living through trials and negative circumstances would not be an occasion for joy.

Choosing to respond to life's difficult situations with inner contentment and satisfaction does not seem to make sense and surely is not a walk in a park.

However, it is the determination to go God's way by remaining true to his word that keeps one joyful.

So joy is a choice that we have to make. The will to make this choice has already been provided by the Lord who is the true source of joy. As we walk with Him, He helps us to experience joy, regardless of what we are going through.

The scripture in Isaiah 12:3 [KJV] says 'Therefore with joy shall ye draw water out of the wells of salvation'. There is also a joy that comes as a result of trials and temptation, the book of James in chapter 1: 2-3 tells us to consider it pure joy when we face trials of many kinds [paraphrased by me].

Simply put, Biblical joy is choosing to respond to external circumstances with an outer expression of inner contentment and satisfaction, because we know that God will use these experiences to accomplish His work in and through our lives. It means saying yes, the situation is this but God says it is okay and I choose to stick with him.

You should also know that with situations thrown at you, this decision will go through cross-examination by the enemy. In a nutshell, your joy will be tested.

I believe you are asking me how, what do I mean by this? Well, I have experienced this test, even recently while I was writing this manuscript. At some point, I lost a whole day's work. It was a huge blow that got me so worked up that I had to scream the name of Jesus when I could not retrieve it.

It was so painful for me. You can imagine the time, energy and emotions put into penning down those words. I had to get out of my house that day to take a walk round the park for an hour while listening to the Word of God as well as praising and worshipping him.

At least that was calming and soothing but I got a double blessing. When I got back to my desk, I had everything to thank God for because, I realised that I still had my laptop, brain and hands to write another one. This assurance gave me the impetus to focus my attention on what next, instead of dwelling on what had happened which was like crying over spilled milk.

I was determined not to allow that circumstance steal my joy because even that momentary exasperation could be so energy draining, which could cost me time and in an extreme case, my health. Now that was true joy expressed there.

There is a flipside to everything on earth. When we describe what Joy is, you can be sure that there is something it is not. Joy is not the feeling that everything in your life is exactly the way you want it at a particular time. This feeling can be called satisfaction or contentment, which is a great feeling in itself but cannot be defined as joy.

Joy is an actual bodily feeling that comes from deep within. When fully experienced, it is physically manifested as there will be an expression of peace and tranquillity around the one who experiences it.

1. How to find joy

Establish in your heart that God is the source of joy.

God is a Spirit and He wants us to "live in the Spirit" and "walk in the Spirit". The Bible says for *'we walk by faith and not by sight;* 2 Corinthians 5: 7[KJV]. This means that He [God] will naturally produce His fruit in our lives as we live for Him. The moment you receive Christ, you are translated from the kingdom of darkness in to light and God's Spirit takes the reins of affairs in your life. Another scripture, Acts 17: 28 [KJV], says, *'for in Him we live and move and have our being, as certain also of your own poets have said, for we are also His offspring'.*

God is the only One that can produce true joy and He does that through His Spirit living in those who have put their trust in Him.

It is important for us to understand that only God can give us the ability to respond to life's difficult circumstances joyfully, while living with those contradictions of life. It is amazing how one can have inner contentment and satisfaction in the midst of chaos and catastrophes.

We can choose to respond to life's trials with joy when we consider God's purpose for those times of suffering.

It is true that only God can supply genuine joy. However, there is a key technique that helps us unlock it. Once again, I need to repeat this verse again, *'My brethren, count it all joy when you fall into various trials knowing that the testing of your faith produces patience, but let patience have its perfect work that you may be perfect and complete lacking nothing'* (James 1:2-4)[NKJV]. You will notice the word "count" in this scripture. That means there will be times and seasons where we must experience these contradictions but those moments will turn out for our good.

The process of learning to respond with joy during times of trials in life must begin with a conscious awareness that God is at work in our lives and that He has a tangible purpose for why we may be experiencing those trials.

In other words, if we have put our faith and trust in Jesus Christ as our own personal saviour and if we believe what His Word teaches us that God is at work in our lives, then we will come to the logical conclusion that trials, suffering, and difficult times in our lives are ultimately designed by God and that He has a specific purpose for us in mind. He says, in Romans 8:28 [KJV], *'and we know that all things work together for good to them that love God, to them who are the called according to His purpose'*.

Notice here, God tests us for promotion but the devil tempts us to fail. When such situations come, we must learn to align with God so as to win and get our promotion rather than fall flat on the ground. We can respond to life's trials with genuine joy if we *understand* that the Lord has a purpose for why He allows those difficult times of suffering and trials to come to us. This passage (Romans 8:28) show us that the purpose of trials is to produce patience or endurance which is the ability to hold up under trials in our lives.

Knowing that our loving Heavenly Father is doing something specific in our lives, which is best for us, helps us respond with genuine joy. Life's trials are certainly not fun, but we can react to those painful situations with joy if we understand that God is demonstrating His love for us through those circumstances. He is an expert in making impossibilities possible to show His might through us. He shows His power, as we hold on to His promises when the enemy thinks he has boxed us in a corner or pushed us to the wall.

If you are in doubt of what I just explained, check out the story of the children of Israel at the Red Sea. God demonstrated what was never expected or seen as possible to save them.

Romans 15:13 [KJV] says, *'Now the God of hope fill you with all joy and peace in believing, that ye may abound in hope, through the power of the Holy Ghost'*. This means that God can fill us with joy and through that joy we can have hope to sail through those trials and temptations.

It is a natural human inclination to think that living through trials and negative circumstances would not be an occasion for joy. Choosing to respond to life's difficult situations with inner contentment and satisfaction does not seem to make sense. Yet, it is possible that the believer can experience genuine joy to the fullest by taking the initiative to actively consider all God is doing and that He has a definite purpose in mind for His people.

Jeremiah 29:11 [KJV] says, '*For I know the thoughts that I think toward you, saith the Lord, thoughts of peace, and not of evil, to give you an expected end*'.

Joy does not mean forcing happiness during sad circumstances. We can usually tell when someone tries to fake it until they make it, which is what the world advises. Joy comes in every season. It is an outpouring of the Holy Spirit. Joy comes when we willingly accept it

CHAPTER 2
This too shall pass

"Heaven and earth shall pass away, but My words will never pass away," Matthew 24:35 [KJV].

Have you felt discouraged or angry at people during those moments of intense trial, when they try to console you by saying words like 'This Too Shall 'Pass, no condition is permanent?

I have heard these words for the most part of my life, but until I became Christian it did not mean anything to me.

I will like to explain it in my understanding, you must accept this truth that it is only God that is permanent and every other thing is subject to change including our situations. I can say that God is the unchangeable Changer, The Alpha and Omega.

No wonder He said, *'weeping may endure for a night, but joy cometh in the morning'* Psalm 30:5b [KJV].

If you check the Bible, God does not refer to the troubles people went through as the issue nor does He talk to His people about their suffering and hard times.

It is not because He is trying to hide them but because He is The Alpha and Omega, Beginning and End, nothing matters in the middle because the end is His destination.

He knows about it and has assured us that when we pass through them, He will be right there with us.

Trials and temptations are not for a few or selected persons, we will and must face them at one point or another in our lives, just as many of us may even find ourselves going through some of them right now.

The great news is this: God never leaves us to fend for ourselves in difficult times. He promises to be with us in all that we encounter. His whole heart encompasses our pain, surrounds us in peace and gives us incredible hope and grace to keep pressing on.

God is eternal and His words stand firm forever. All of us, as believers, are promised eternal life with Him, once we are redeemed and made new. So, In the midst of our most trying and painful times, these are the truths that should give us hope and strength.

2 Corinthians 4:16-18 [KJV] says, 'for which cause we faint not, but though our outward man perish, yet the inward man is renewed day by day. For our light affliction, which is but for a moment, worketh for us a far more exceeding and eternal weight of glory. While we look not at the things which are seen, but at the things which are not seen. For the things which are seen are temporal, but the things which are not seen are eternal'.

As believers in Christ, we can hold fast to this promise. We have an eternal destiny through Him. God will never waste the pain we face in this life. He will turn it around for good - every battle, every hard place, every dark time and every painful storm. He will never allow us to walk through deep struggle without allowing it to bring greater hope and purpose, both in our own lives and in the lives of those we are called to in this world.

The trial itself will not label us as many will want to believe when deceived by the enemy.

We are defined by our Lord Himself who saved us by lifts us out of the deep, who brings us through the fire, who takes us straight out of the darkness into greater purpose and blessing up our ahead.

1Peter 2:9 (KJV) says, *'But ye are a Chosen Generation, a royal priesthood, an holy nation, a peculiar people; that ye should shew forth the praises of him who hath called us out of darkness into His marvellous light'*. In other words, we are restored, redeemed and renewed, from any circumstances we find ourselves in.

Hear, what He says again, in John 16:33 (KJV)

"These things I have spoken unto you, that in me ye might have peace. In the world ye shall have tribulation: but be of good cheer; I have overcome the world".

Jesus reminds us that there will be trouble in this world, and we can surely expect it, not as those who go looking for it but we will be target of the enemy. However the good news is that He has already overcome it all. The scripture says *'Thanks be to God, who gives us the victory through our Lord Jesus Christ'* 1 Corinthians 15:57[NKJV].

The Believer actually fights from the point of Victory.

He is already victorious, the same victory is ours and that power works in us today, giving us the courage and strength, we need to persevere and overcome.

One of my darkest times was when I lost my parents within the space of three years. It was unbelievable. I suddenly became an orphan when I was least prepared for it. You may ask me, can anyone ever prepare for a death of a loved one? That is a big question that is difficult to answer. The death of a loved one always comes with a heartache that only the joy of the Lord can take one through. Indeed one's strength cannot prevail in such situations.

My heart was broken, especially after the death of my dad, as my mum passed on first. I was taking consolation in the fact that my father was still alive and I promised to make sure I showered him with all that I could not shower on mum before she passed. Since I was unable to fulfil all of those my heart's desires before my father passed on, I was broken. It was a very dark period for me, but as it turned out, something good came out of it which was the birth of my first book titled "Help My Heart".

The book was written with tears and a broken heart. It however, set the stage for my writing career. Over five hundred copies were printed in November 2007 and distributed free to everyone that attended his funeral service. Glory!

I did not allow that circumstance to define my joy. I refused to waste my pain instead it became the fuel for the energy I needed to write the book.

Now, what about you? When all is said and done, do you want to look back and give glory to God? Will you be able to say "through it all, through it all, I have learnt to trust in Jesus, I have learnt to trust in God", the God of all comfort, the Ever Present One in times of trouble?

For every trial and season of suffering we encounter in life; God wants to use it to make a mark in this world. The troubles we walk through can bring glory to Him. He will use our lives, joy and faith to draw others to Himself, despite our problems. He will help us to remember that what we see around us is not all that there is to it, for He has more in store and it is greater than what we can ever imagine.

May His Presence surround you in the hard places you might be facing right now, and may He lead you and keep you secure, guiding your steps forward and covering you from behind.

As Job 23:10 says 'but He knoweth the way that I take, when He hath tried me, I shall come forth as gold'.

He knows your way and calls you by name. This shows that He knows us individually.

2.1. Accept the situation

A friend shared her story with me. In her words - *when I discovered that I was pregnant I was extremely happy. However, four months into the pregnancy, after a vigil at a church service, my water broke and I was rushed to a hospital. The doctor was unable to diagnose why the water broke; a number of tests were conducted, but they returned negative.*

We were informed that the fluid would not be replaced and that if we did not terminate the pregnancy my life would be in danger. We decided to trust God and I was at peace.

Interestingly, God had spoken to me a few months before that there was going to be a big storm in my life, but He had overcome the storm. So when that happened, this prophecy enabled me to weather the storm. I was placed on bed rest for two months. I was literally not moving about, unless I had to use the bathroom or go to the hospital for a check-up.

At some point in time, during a time of prayer, I went into labour and was rushed to the hospital. We lost the baby at six months. I did not question God because He did overcome the storm. Although, I lost my baby, God preserved my life. I know that my baby is in heaven enjoying the presence of God.

I had joy knowing that God is always with me regardless of the outcome. Testimonies abound of people who have visited heaven testifying that there is a place for babies lost through miscarriage. Heaven is more real than the earth. This was and is my joy.

The joy of the Lord is not just restricted to when good things happen to us. A song writer wrote ''the God of the good times, is the God in the bad times' how succinct. The joy of the Lord was my strength and kept me going when I was in that storm. God has not promised that we will not have challenges, but He does promise that He will make away of escape for every one of them. From my friend's story you can see that she accepted the situation and received God's comfort which kept her joy.

2.2 Perspective: what we become with acceptance

One of the reasons that suffering can be valuable is because after the experience, people can say with conviction, "I know how you feel. I've been in your shoes." Suffering prepares us to minister comfort to others who suffer. God's intention actually, is that we comfort one another through our experiences.

The feeling of isolation is one of the hardest parts of suffering. It can make you feel like you are all alone in your pain. The comfort of those who have known and gone through that same pain is inexpressible.

Recently, I started a new job as civil servant. Initially, I was not sure if there was anyone in a similar situation as I am (hearing impaired or deaf). Guess what? As I was carrying out a research, I came across a group that was formed specifically for people with hearing loss. What a relief! Immediately I made myself known and joined the group.

Little did I know that I was not alone in my situation. What am I saying here? Find and join a group, people or setting that relate to your situation, so that you can make a difference. Per adventure there is none, then why can't you start one? You never know, you might be a light in someone's dark world.

There is another aspect of bringing comfort to those in pain. It is highly unlikely that those who have suffered will judge others experiencing a similar suffering. This is a great comfort to those who hurt. When you are in pain, your world narrows down to mere survival as being judged would only add salt to the injury.

Pain is inevitable because we live in a fallen world, it reminds us that we are "destined for trials." We do not have a choice as to whether we will suffer or not, our choice is to go through it by ourselves or with God. As children of God, it is very important that we see beyond our pain by seeing the hope that will be revealed in it, just as the scripture says concerning Jesus, for the joy that was set before him, Christ endured the suffering of dying on the cross. That was not an easy task, but He had to surrender to the will of the Father and went through it.

We can go through our life challenges as well, with our eyes fixed on the joy that will be revealed to us later.

"For which cause we faint not; but though our outward man is renewed day by day. For our light affliction, which is but for a moment, worketh for us a far more exceeding and eternal weight of glory; while we look not at the things which are not seen: for the things which are seen are temporal; but the things which are not seen are eternal" 2 Corinthians 4:16-18(KJV).

2.3 His power works within us

"But we have this treasure in jars of clay to show that this all-surpassing power is from God and not from us. We are

hard pressed on every side, but not crushed; perplexed, but not in despair; persecuted, but not abandoned; struck down, but not destroyed," 2 Corinthians 4:7-9 [NIV].

One of the most miraculous reminders of God's constant loving care over us is this: He has given us the spirit of his very presence. He is with us, continually. Though we may forget, he never does. He fights for us. He carries us. He strengthens us. He protects us. He covers us. He leads us. At times, we may not even be aware of the incredible ways he is working even within our times of greatest need.

If you are hurting today, be rest assured that God has not forgotten you. He sees the pain you have carried and offers you the peace and security of his very presence rising up within you. Do not ever feel like you have got to face things on your own. As believers, we have "this treasure" within us and we will not be crushed! When we belong to Jesus, no amount of suffering we endure can hold the power over us. He is greater than all we face. His word says *'Greater is He that is in me than he that is in the world'* 1 John 4:4b [KJV].

CHAPTER 3

Count your blessings

3.1 What is Gratitude?

Gratitude is very important character or attitude we must imbibe in order to have the real joy. It is learning to say thank you for the littlest or seemingly inconsequential thing done for us.

In Christianity, gratitude is basically an acknowledgment of God's generosity. This attitude inspires Christians to shape their thoughts and actions. Christian gratitude is not just a sentimental feeling but is regarded as a virtue that shapes emotions, thoughts, actions and deeds.

On the flipside, ingratitude was at the heart of the fall of man and is still at the heart of what is fallen about us to this day. *"Although they knew God, they did not glorify Him as God nor were they thankful". Romans 1:21 [NKJV]*

Again and again throughout the Old Testament, especially in the Psalms, we see that gratitude to God that is the best response to His gracious acts of deliverance. Any wonder that God called David a man after His heart, despite his shortcomings?

Christ's sacrificial death and triumphant resurrection elicits profound gratitude, among other things, from the heart of a born-again Christian. In the daily Christian life, it is the genuine gratitude for God's gifts that keeps us from idolatry and sinful life.

With the growing demand of activities in our lives, it is easy to forget to thank God for His daily benefits towards us. I encourage you to make intentional efforts to slow down, take stock and express gratitude to the glory of God.

To have joy, we need to count our many blessings, name them one by one. Particularly, thank Him for what you have. Often times we concentrate on only what we do not have and the devil magnifies them leaving us with the feeling of ingratitude.

I remember when the loss of my hearing started, I made a conscious effort to thank God for my eyes. I am blessed with beautiful eyes and I have relied on it so much to compensate for my hearing loss. Also, my sense of smell is quite strong. There was a day that toasted bread was burning in my kitchen and no one realised it, despite the fact that I was far away from the kitchen, I could smell it even before the smoke alarm went off. Is that not a blessing? People used to ask me to read the small print of writings for them as my eyes were so sharp though it is getting a bit tired now due to the pressure of reading a lot and other use. Yet, I am very grateful to God for my hearing, though not perfect but I thank Him for provision of hearing aids. I can still enjoy the sound of birds in my garden especially during summer when I open my window for ventilation.

3.2 Where is the gratitude in this?

"Give thanks to the Lord, for he is good, his love endures forever." (Psalm 136:1, NIV)

I need to reiterate that gratitude is the heart of the Christian life. "Gratitude may be the best measure of our spirituality." Why is this? Because gratitude demonstrates that we have been paying attention to the gifts we received. Especially the gift of grace we have received in Jesus Christ. This is so profound.

So, if gratitude is so important, it begs the questions: Am I grateful? What am I grateful for? I recall when I was losing my hearing, I could not see anything to thank God for. Apparently, the devil lied to me and made me bitter but when the eyes of my understanding were open, I began thanking God for His mercy upon my life because it could have been worse. I remember the story of Madam Helen Keller, a woman who did great exploits and left legacies even after almost two centuries. She lost her sight and hearing, yet she had something to be thankful for. So, in my case, I thought, what if there was no sound left for hearing aids to work with? Or, what if I had woken up one morning and I am pronounced deaf and dumb? What would I have done?

If God opens our eyes to see the battles that He fights for us, we will have every reason to be grateful. So, may I ask, what are you grateful for? Identify just one thing. If you think deeper, there will be a lot more to outlast the ones not yet done.

Gratitude takes nothing for granted. It acknowledges each favour and gift, both big and small. It also recognizes the giver, for instance the relative who shows her love by giving you a gift; the friend who remembers to call you and even the stranger that gives you a lift when you were on a lonely road with no means of transport in sight.

If we stop to think about it, we have received a lot of gifts from many people, especially from God. We have a lot to be thankful for. However, often we are too busy to see it. Have you stopped to thank God for the gifts he has given you, especially the gift of grace in Jesus Christ?

I have come to realise the fact that when I am becoming stressed out and complaining it is because my bank of thankfulness is running low. So, I submit to you that whenever you are becoming a complainer, stop and assess your heart. Ask yourself "where is the gratitude in this?" Find it and you will see that there is a lot to be grateful for. Be grateful for what He has done and what He is doing in your life. Our reasons for thanking God should not be only for what we have or do not have but for who He is.

You might ask, how can you be grateful in your hopeless situation? It is just a mind-set. All you need to do is think of those things that glorify God. Keep a gratitude journal or daily diary that focuses on the blessings in your life. Take stock, no matter how small they are, overtime, they will add up and you will have something to look back on and be grateful for.

The devil's stock in trade is to keep making us look the other way, seeking for what is not there. His subtle question still remains as he asked Eve in the Garden of Eden, 'did God say?' Often times we overlook what God has done for us, thinking it is not big enough. Resist the devil and he will flee. That is what the Book of James 4:7b [KJV] says.

If we can see God working behind the scenes of our lives and know that He is working all things together for our good including our suffering, pain, trials and shortcomings, then we will be grateful.

Let me tell you another story. Once, I was in a situation where my employment was terminated on the spot without prior notice. It made me so bitter and sad, causing me to feel overwhelmed that I could not see beyond the disappointment. I could not even nurture the thought of any blessing coming out of it. However, as time went on, I saw better and looking back now, indeed I can testify that all things work together for my good as God has done tremendous things in my life including self-development, character development and spiritual development. God has a way of working such situations out for our good.

God does not only have great things in store for us in the future, but also works now through our sufferings for our good. *'For we know that for those who love God all things work together for good, for those who are called according to his purpose'* Romans 8:28 [KJV].

Suffering allows us to minister comfort

I would like to reiterate that one of the reasons sufferings is valuable is because after the experience, people can say with conviction, "I know how you feel. I've been in your shoes." This just shows that what you might be going through now is beyond you but if you can trust God to take you through, some day you will be a comfort to many more that will pass through a similar situation.

So, putting it straight, our suffering prepares us to minister comfort to others who will suffer later.

Feeling isolated is one of the hardest parts of suffering. It can feel like you are all alone in your pain and that makes it worse. The comfort of those who have known that same pain is inexpressible. For someone to say those powerful words, "I know just how you feel because I've been there" that person must have had to walk through the same difficult valley first.

I dare say, your pain is not always about you. It may well be about other people, preparing you to minister comfort and hope to someone in your future who will need what you can give them because of what you are going through right now.

We are the extension of God's hand on earth. God cannot come again to live physically with us as he did through Jesus. We are His express image and can do what He did through Christ that strengthens us.

I can confidently tell you that, my story of hearing impairment is changing lives all over the world through my book and ministry. If you are faithful enough to cling to God now, I promise He will use you greatly to comfort others later. If you have this perspective about your suffering, you will know that your suffering is not pointless but for a purpose which is yet to be revealed.

There is another aspect of bringing comfort to those in pain. When you are in pain it is easy for others to judge you for not "following the rules". That should only apply to those whose lives are not being swallowed by the painful event.

Have you not read the story in the bible where the Lord Jesus said to his disciples that the blindness of the young man who was blind from birth was not as a result of his sin but that God should be glorified through him? Was God glorified? Oh yes, because that singular miracle added to the fulfilment of Jesus' purpose on earth.

Suffering often develops compassion and mercy in us. Those who suffer tend to have tender hearts toward others who are in pain. It gives us the wider perspective to life, so we can comfort others with the comfort that we have received from God (2 Corinthians 1:4) because we have experienced the reality of the Holy Spirit being there for us, walking alongside us in our pain. Then we can turn around and walk alongside others in their pain, showing the compassion that our own suffering has produced in us.

Suffering is also excellent at teaching us humble dependence on God, the only appropriate response to our Creator. Ever since the fall of Adam, we keep forgetting that God created us to depend on Him and not on ourselves. We keep desiring to go our own way, pretending that we are God. Suffering is powerfully able to get us back on track. It is like applying the brakes when driving non-stop on a highway, it slows or even stops us on a track of self-drive. If you catch my drift, I'm referring to the "me, myself and I" syndrome which many of us have running in our lives. At such points you accept that you are helpless without God.

I have come to know in my life that without the power of the Holy Spirit, I cannot do anything. I am totally dependent on Him.

Sometimes we hurt so much we cannot pray. We are forced to depend on the intercession of the Holy Spirit and the saints, needing them to go before the throne of God on our behalf. Instead of seeing that inability to pray as a personal failure, we can rejoice that our perception of being totally needy corresponds to the truth that we really are that needy.

"But we had the sentence of death in ourselves that we should not trust in ourselves, but in God which raiseth the dead" 2 Corinthians 1:9 [KJV].

As painful as it is, suffering strips away the distractions of life as we are forced to face the fact that we are powerless to change other people and most situations. For instance, we can have all the money to take a loved one who is critically ill to the best hospital with all the world's best medical facilities, but healing remains God's prerogative. Such situation leaves us to focus on asking God for mercy.

The fear that accompanies suffering drives us to the Father like a little kid burying his face in his father's lap. Recognizing our own powerlessness is the key to experiencing real power because we must acknowledge our dependence on God before His power can flow from His heart into our lives.

The day I surrendered my hearing loss completely to God, was the day I was humiliated and embarrassed beyond measure. I was asked to do one thing, but I did the opposite. When I was told later that what I was asked to do was totally different from what I did, I cried to the Lord to take away my shame and inability to hear and put an end to embarrassment in my life. That was the day I decided to exchange my disability for God's ability.

I trusted the Lord to turn my situation around for good. He is still working and knitting every experience, hardship, and my life challenges for His glory. He would not permit what I cannot handle to come upon me. Even when it happens, He will always make a way of escape. I have learnt to depend on God, knowing that without Him I cannot do anything.

I encourage you to also ask Him what He would have you do with what He gave you.

How could you use your God-given gifts to give back to others? I do not believe God gives us talents for ourselves. I believe he gives them to us so we can serve others and show them the love of Christ. After all, that is our job here on earth. It is all about keeping it in the right perspective. The same goes for our suffering and pain. My pain of losing my hearing has enabled me to understand what it means to be disabled and in need of aids to be able to function well. Through it I have been able to offer encouragement and support to others going through similar life's challenges. The joy of being there for others during their life's challenges cannot be over emphasised especially when they are able to find joy as well during their difficult times.

CHAPTER 4
Humility

I know that you have come across this saying, 'pride goes before a fall'. It is a common saying but it is least taken cognisance of because many great men and women have fallen victims to the spirit of pride which led to their mighty fall.

The first creature who lost his estate as a result of pride was the devil himself. He was formerly known as Lucifer, the angel of light. Ezekiel 28: 12-13, 15 & 17[KJV] explains this fully:

[12] 'Son of man take up a lamentation upon the king of Tyre, and say unto him, thus saith the Lord God, thou sealest up the sum, full of wisdom and perfect in beauty.

[13] Thou has been in Eden the garden of God, every precious stone was thy covering, the sardius, topaz and diamond, the beryl, the onyx and the jasper, the sapphire, the carbuncle and gold, the workmanship of thy tabrets and of thy pipes was prepared in thee in the day that thou was created…

[15] Thou was perfect in thy ways from the day thou was created till iniquity was found in thee.

17 Thine heart was lifted up because of thy beauty, thou hast corrupted thy wisdom by reason of thy brightness, I will cast thee to the ground, I will lay thee before kings, that they may behold thee'.

This scripture humbles me whenever I read it. Meditate on the beauty, splendour and gifts lavished on Lucifer. One would have thought that those resources will cost God so much that He would have considered allowing him to stay back, but then he still cast him out. This goes to show that God has zero tolerance for lack of humility.

We cannot bribe Him with wealth because cattle of a thousand hills are His and His store house is inexhaustible.

In our pathway to joy, humility is required. I once thought that I was humble person however, I had more understanding of what humility is about during my personal trial of losing my hearing. During that period, I was offered a pair of hearing aids, but pride did not allow me to accept it. My initial thought was that I would rather let God heal me naturally than use hearing aids. Yes, that was good but deep down within me, I was feeling too righteous to accept man made solutions. This is how a lot of us behave, we have our mind set on how God should answer our prayers.

We must establish in our hearts that God loves humility and hates pride. For all those who exalt themselves will be humbled and those who humble themselves will be exalted. In another bible passage it says, 'but He giveth more grace. Wherefore he saith, God resisteth the proud, but giveth grace unto the humble' James 4:6 [KJV].

There are so many people out there that are suffering and would not open up to receive support, instead, they would rather put up a pretence and say that they are believing God for such miracle. Those are the people that would not admit they need help from people they feel they are more important than. It could be because of their positions in the church, place of work or the society generally. However, God wants us to humble ourselves so that He can exalt us in due course. In humbling ourselves we receive the peace and joy of God.

We can pray like Apostle Paul who talks to the Corinthian believers about all the hardships he had been through on the missionary trip with his team. Paul understood the power of prayer and was not pretending in the face of difficulties. He recognised that there was a battle going on in the heavenlies which required a different kind of prayer and he asked for it, refusing to suffer in silence. How many believers are going through trials but self-righteousness would not let them open up and receive support and prayer. The devil lies to many that if they open up, they will be disgraced by the whole world. The fact is this: the reverse is the case. If they keep silent the whole world will eventually hear and even see it.

Some would not accept medication as it was in my own case. I would not accept the hearing aid, till I was embarrassed because I was unable to follow through a conversation especially in a large congregation. This went on for years till I humbled myself and received the support I needed. That was when I was flooded with the joy of God like a river as the scripture says and I went on to be a blessing to others as I share my story.

2 Corinthians 1:8-11[KJV] says *8 'For we would not, brethren, have you ignorant of our trouble which came to us in Asia, 9But we had the sentence of death in ourselves, that we should not trust in ourselves, but in God which raiseth the dead, 10Who delivered us from so great a death, and doth deliver, in whom we trust that He will yet deliver us, 11Ye*

also helping together by prayer for us, that for the gift bestowed upon us by the means of many persons thanks may be given by many on my behalf'.

Paul believed that as they were on this journey, forceful men among the Corinthian believers were laying hold of the battle, standing in the gap through prayer and that prayer had a profound impact on what was literally happening! Paul, when encouraging people to join in prayer, writes in Romans 15:30 [KJV] *'Now I beseech you, brethren, for the Lord Jesus Christ's sake, and for the love of the Holy Spirit, that ye strive together with me in your prayers to God for me'.*

4:1 God honours humility

When I eventually humbled myself, God exalted me and He is now using me to make impact in the lives of others. I am no longer bowing down my head in shame rather, I look up to God and I look around to see who I can be a blessing to. My life has become an overflowing river of joy to others.

Lack of humility delays advancement, we must watch out for it and always pray like David who prayed a very powerful prayer in Psalm 139: 23-24 [KJV] *'Search me, O God and know my heart, try me, and know my thoughts and see if there be any wicked way in me, and lead me in the way everlasting'.*

Chapter 5

Power of Intercession

I do not consider myself an expert on prayer, however, one of the benefits that I have experienced when standing with others in prayer is the birth of hope and joy. Assuring people that all will be well, can change their countenance instantly.

Even when the situation does not turn out as expected, the fact that they know someone is standing in the gap for them gives them some peace and joy.

Prayer has birthed a new perspective in me that has personally increased my faith, I am not just asking for prayer, but the question is now directed to others "How can I pray for you?" This is because I have discovered that it is a privilege and joy to stand with others in their difficult times and see God do what He knows best.

Praying for others has been a balm to my soul as well. In most cases, when I found myself unable to pray as I should, others are busying praying for me because of the seeds I have sown.

This is so soothing; it produces a joyful feeling knowing that I am not alone in my situation and that I have people also standing in the gap for me. When we give, one way or the other, it surely comes back to us. In most cases when you pray for others, you will also feel a great joy welling up in your heart knowing it is the will of God.

A great example is seen in the life of Apostle Paul. While he was in prison, he always prayed for the churches and individuals because the testimonies that came out of such selfless service, gave him joy and sincere thanksgiving to God which encouraged him to carry on praying for them. If Paul who was in chains and in prison (not the regular ones we have today, his was a dungeon), could pray for the churches that were not in prison, what other excuse do we have as free people who are not gagged or locked up somewhere?

We can use our situation to advance and build the kingdom of God and while doing that we too we will testify that it gives us joy to see others being empowered and encouraged through our prayer for and with them.

Ephesians 6:18[KJV] Paul admonished that *'praying always with all prayer and supplication in the Spirit*

and watching thereunto with all perseverance and supplication for all saints'.

CHAPTER 6

Staying in God's Presence

God's presence can bring us fullness of joy and as a matter of fact, His presence has the fullness of joy. Psalm 16:11[KJV] says, '*In Your presence is fullness of joy; At Your right hand are pleasures forevermore'*.

This passage is in essence saying that when we abide in Jesus Christ, it is absolutely expected that joy flows into us. That does not mean that everything will be alright and that troubles will not come at some points in our lives, but that even amidst hardships, the Bible speaks endlessly about the abundance of joy that comes with God's Spirit.

If you are dismayed, depressed, struggling to find hope and get your vibrancy back, never forget to run to God and seek His joy that is promised like the rising of the sun.

It is better to fall into the hands of God than the hands of the enemies. I am glad that, when life's difficulty pushes me I always run back to God. I have come to learn that regardless of my shortcomings, He will always accept me, this has given me great comfort and joy. There is no better place to be whether when I am happy or sad. His presence is where I always want to be.

What about you? Will you allow your situation to draw you closer to God or drive you away from Him?

Another song writer wrote these beautiful lyrics, "you're all I want, you're all I've ever needed..." No matter how tough it is, God is all you need.

In Psalm 139:8-10[KJV], the Psalmist says *'if I ascend up into heaven, thou art there, if I make my bed in hell, behold thou art there. If I take the wings of the morning and dwell in the uttermost parts of the sea, even there thy hand lead me and thy right hand shall hold me'.*

During my difficult time, I was tempted to stay away from church. However, I always heard that voice saying - do not miss the day of your visitation. I should realise that what the enemy wanted was to cut me off from the presence of other believers and God which is a dangerous place to be as staying at home robs me of the strength and comfort of God. It robs me of an opportunity to be a testimony of God's goodness. It also robs others of the chance to see how a Christian handles a severe trial while hanging in there in faith.

My presence demonstrates to the powers of darkness that I worship God because of Who He is, not because of what He gives me. I believe a hurting, sorrowing Christian who has resolved to go to church and worship no matter what, can be a source of hope to others who are, or who soon will be, in a season of trial and difficulties because we will all pass through it.

Psalm 27:4 [KJV], says *'one thing have I desired one the Lord. That will I seek after, that I may dwell in the house of The Lord all the days of my life to behold the beauty of the Lord and to inquire of His temple'*.

So, ask the Lord for grace and strength to honour Him by worshipping Him in the assembly of His people, even when it hurts. Worship that means something, costs something. Be a good soldier. Worship is what we should do whether we are happy or not, because that is our essence of living for Him there lies the source of our unlimited joy.   .

6.1 How the Word of God brings joy

"Jeremiah 15:16 [KJV] says, *'Thy words were found, and I did eat them, and Thy word was unto me the joy and rejoicing of mine heart; for I am called by Thy name, O LORD God of hosts.'*

Psalm 19:7[BSB] adds, *'The law of The Lord is perfect, reviving the soul, the testimony of The Lord is sure making wise the simple'.*

Psalm 19:10 [KJV] says, *'More to be desired are they than gold even much fine gold sweeter also than honey in the honey comb.'*

Do you know that there is joy in just reading the Bible?

Revelation 1:3 [KJV] says *'Blessed is he that readeth and they that hear the words of this prophecy and keep those things which are written therein; for the time is at hand'.*

These scriptures just show us other ways of finding genuine joy through God's word.

I am so grateful for the joy I find in God's Word, each time I turn to it. Indeed it has been wonderful to know that the Word of God never expires, nor does it need an update. During my most challenging time, I always found comfort in the Word of God, when all other things failed, the Word of God remained my anchor.

At the time that I was diagnosed of losing my hearing, I keyed into the Word of God for His promises. I ate it, lived it, spoke it, walked and expressed it in every way possible to keep me on track. Although my hearing function has not been fully restored as it should be, however, the comfort and the assurance of God's Word has given me hope and peace, knowing fully well that one day my joy would be full regarding my hearing.

The good thing about the Word of God is that when you are standing on it, it empowers you. You never get an overdose of it and to cap it up, it has no side effect.

Confessing God's Word is a way of assuring yourself of who you are and what you have in Christ. It helps you to live free of the devil's devices and develop a joyful life.

In my book "Exchanging My Disability for God's Ability" I dedicated a whole chapter to confessing your way out of disabling and limiting thoughts with God's enabling and empowering promises.

The Psalmist says, *'Thy word is a lamp unto my feet and a light unto path my path'* (Psalm 119:105, KJV). When your path is illuminated, it means that you know where you are headed. There is no way you will not be joyful because darkness itself brings sadness.

CHAPTER 7

Forgiveness

7.1 What is forgiveness?

In your quest for the real Joy, I have been talking about in the last six chapters, another thing you must develop or ask God to help you is to have forgiveness.

Forgiveness is the commitment to a personalised process of change. By moving from suffering to forgiveness, you will improve your life and enrich the life of others around you. Forgiveness means different things to different people. Generally, however, it involves a decision to let go of resentment and thoughts of revenge.

Mathew 6: 14-15 [KJV] *'For if ye forgive men their trespasses, your heavenly Father will also forgive you but if ye forgive not men their trespasses, neither will your Father forgive your trespasses'.*

These two verses encapsulate forgiveness as releasing whoever offended you from blame, leaving it in the hands of God and moving on with your life.

From the Bible's perspective, forgiveness is a command, not just an admonition.

7.2 How can Forgiveness help my situation?

I hear people say I forgive but cannot forget and others say it is impossible to forgive completely especially when the pain cuts so deeply.

I am not here to judge but to help us see that it is very possible from the Christian perspective.

Our Lord and Saviour, Jesus Christ is the perfect example of forgiveness. He demonstrated this on the cross while in agonising pain for a crime He did not commit and choosing to die the most debasing of all deaths.

Sometimes people are stuck and depressed because they struggle with forgiveness. Sometimes it is even towards themselves thus they lose their joy and more often than not, develop complicated medical issues that could terminate their lives eventually.

Being hurt by someone, particularly someone you love and trust, can cause anger, sadness and confusion. If you dwell on hurtful events or situations, grudges filled with resentment, vengeance and hostility can take root. If we allow negative feelings to crowd out positive feelings, we might find ourselves swallowed up by our own bitterness or sense of injustice.

Some people are naturally more forgiving than others but even if you are a grudge-holder by your temperament, you can learn to be more forgiving.

When you are holding a grudge, you can be sure that joy cannot flow through you at the same time, you can only have one or the other. Unfortunately, in that state you only open yourself to the work of the devil.

Sooner or later, you become so wrapped up in the wrong that you cannot enjoy the presence of God, this can result in depression as you begin to isolate yourself. It is a dangerous place to be. Instead, learn to let go and remain in the presence of God where there is unlimited joy.

Let me make it clear here that I do not mean that you fail to acknowledge the wrong done to you, by all means, do not deny the wrong or your hurt, acknowledge your emotions about the harm done to you and how they affect you but owe it to yourself to release the negative emotions and let it go for your personal benefit.

You might say it is easier said than done, I agree, but it does not mean that it cannot be done. Forgiveness can be challenging, at times especially if the person who caused the hurt doesn't admit his or her wrong doing.

If you find yourself stuck with such, you can practice empathy. One of the ways that I deal with forgiveness is to forgive in advance, before offence comes. Sometimes, I make excuses for people by saying I forgive them because they do not know what they are doing or saying. Clue from Jesus statement on the cross, He said, 'Father forgive them, for they do not know what they do' (Luke 23:24, NKJV).

Sometimes forgiveness can be a process and even small hurts may need to be revisited and forgiven, over and over again. Do I say it is easy? Not all, but the benefits are immeasurable. In my book titled, "Exchanging my Disability for God's Ability, I devoted a chapter to dealing with issues of forgiveness and how it can bring about healing and unlimited joy.

Remember you are not forgiving others because you want them to change their actions or behaviours. That is not the point or the purpose. Think about forgiveness, more of how it can change your life by bringing you peace, happiness, emotional and spiritual healing. Forgiveness can take away the power the other person exerts on your life. By this I mean, that feeling of fear and rush of negative emotions that comes upon you once that person appears or when your mind flashes back to the event, does not control you anymore.

Many actually turn down invitations to valuable meetings because they do not want to run into that person that offended them. Doing that gives the person power over you, so get it back by releasing the person from your heart.

It is also crucial to remember that you cannot force someone to forgive you. Others need to forgive in their own time. Nevertheless, you can commit to treating others with respect, compassion and empathy.

7.3 Joy in the midst of setbacks

Here is another story shared by my friend. *Growing up was not a pleasant experience for me because of the child abuse I suffered from the age of eight. I was miserable in those days and very unhappy. I lost my self-esteem and confidence. This affected me even up till adulthood. However, I experienced the Joy of the Lord in various ways when I gave my life to Christ at the age of thirteen. It was a joyful experience and I still remember how peaceful and joyful I felt internally. The unpleasant experiences I went through did not stop as a number of other experiences happened thereafter, but what I found out was that joy and happiness are two different experiences. Happiness comes when we receive things we desire. For instance, I am happy when God answers my prayer for a new job. On the other hand, he has not answered my prayer for breakthrough in my finances. This may not make me happy, but I still remain joyful.*

How is that possible? It is possible to be joyful even if you do not have what you desire because Joy comes from the Lord. It is a fruit of the Spirit according to Galatians 5:22 [KJV] says; 'But the fruit of The Spirit is love, joy, peace, longsuffering, gentleness, goodness, faith'.

Joy once given, can be permanent if you hold onto it tenaciously. I have resolved that I will not trade it for anything nor will I allow circumstances of life to tamper with it. Joy is real and for a child of God, this sets us above the unbelievers. We should always remain positive and see lights at the end of each tunnel that each season of life brings to us, no matter the situation. Today, I can boldly say that God has changed my story. I no longer feel pain from my past experiences because God has given me a new song. I now use my story to help women all over the world to heal

from their own pain through the "Inner Healing Course"
which I run together with a wonderful sister in the Lord.

I am grateful to God for helping me find Joy in the midst of
my setback".

Kikelomo Adebiyi

Co-founder Rapha Nurturing Academy

CHAPTER 8

Praise

8.1 God loves our sacrifice of praise

A sacrifice is an offering to one considered as a higher being in our case here it is to God. It entails giving our best to the One whom we love and serve. The only sacrifices mentioned in the New Testament are the sacrifices of praise, thanksgiving and joy.

"By Him therefore let us offer the sacrifice of praise to our God continually God a sacrifice of praise – the fruit of lips that openly profess his name. But to do good and to communicate forget not, for with such sacrifices God is well pleased." Hebrews 13:15-16 [KJV]

One example of how praise can be turned for good that will eventually bring us lasting joy is when we use it as a battle axe. 2 Chronicles 20:17 [KJV] says *'Ye shall not need to fight in this battle, set yourselves, stand ye still, and see the salvation of The Lord with you o Judah and Jerusalem fear not, nor be dismayed, tomorrow go out against them, for the Lord will be with you'.*

The children of Israel were facing the most difficult time in their history. Armies that were by every human standard more powerful than them were fighting against them but by the leading of God they conquered. They exercised the power of praise, the most unlikely weapon. This is a perfect example of using praise as a battle axe.

Imagine being asked to praise instead of defending yourself when an aggressive opponent is approaching you, what will your response be? The one giving the advice will be termed insane but that was what they did and got the victory.

Let me share another story with you, this time around, a personal story. During one of my most challenging times, someone very dear and close to me took ill. It was God that saw us through by His Word, Prayer and Praise. I had the revelation of the power of praise and immediately I confessed that it would end in praise. Although at a point it was really bad, humanly speaking, ordinarily one would have expected a different outcome. However, the Word of God cannot return to him void.

God says we should pray and He will answer. He also said that He inhabits our praises. God is too faithful to fail in any situation. I can testify that at the end, the whole situation ended in praise. My beloved was made whole, to God alone be the glory. Hallelujah.

Have you prayed, given your time, sown seeds and professed the word yet it seems like that situation will not change? Try the sacrifice of praise.

It is a sacrifice; it will take a lot from you. It might place you in the eyes of people as stupid but hang in there. God's greatest 'Food' as a man of God puts it, is praise. He cannot resist a sacrificial praise that comes from a contrite heart.

Expect your joy to be full.

CHAPTER 9

Attaining this Joy

9.1 How do I receive this unlimited joy?

In the preceding eight chapters, I explained the concepts of joy and happiness as well as the difference between them. With the help of the Holy Ghost, we also established how you can also sustain joy as a Christian. However, I do not want to assume that everyone reading this book is a Christian. I also do not want to assume that, as a Christian reading this book, you have not lost your joy.

There are times you find out that you have lost joy in your life due to the cares of life. You no longer seem excited or happy, even with some positive things happening around you. For an unbeliever, without sounding condescending I can authoritatively tell you that you cannot even find joy until you encounter The One who is the joy Giver.

The Lord Jesus is the joy giver. In fact, He is the source of joy. You can ask Him to restore the joy in your heart or give you joy as you receive and accept Him into your life as your Lord and Saviour. Ask Him to fill you with gladness, and He will gladly do that for you. Whenever, I am tempted to feel grumpy, I quickly return to my source, Jesus Christ, the joy giver.

You shall walk in that joy or gladness despite what is happening in and around your life. That joy will sail you through stormy seasons. Friend, ask and it shall be given to you so you will know how to laugh again.

God's plan is for you is to have a life full of joy and not sorrow. Although you will go through seasons of hardships and struggles, you can rest knowing that God's plan for you is good even when things look bad.

Psalm 16:11 [KJV], says, *'Thou wilt shew me the path of life, in Thy presence is fullness of joy, at Thy right hand there are pleasures for evermore.'*

Seek God's presence in the midst of your struggles and you will find yourself filled with His joy. God's presence always follows with His joy. So, remember, joy is attainable.

True Joy comes from the presence of God. Psalms 16:8-11 [KJV] says, *'I have set the LORD always before me, because He is at my right hand I shall not be moved. Therefore my heart is glad, and my glory rejoiceth; my flesh also shall rest in hope. For Thou will not leave my soul in hell, neither wilt Thou suffer thine Holy One to see corruption. Thou wilt shew me the path of life, in Thy presence is fullness of joy, at Thy right hand there are pleasures forevermore'.*

So how do you begin? One quick and fast way to get long lasting joy is service. You know how to do that by recognizing your purpose in life.

You may be asking now "How do I serve?" I will show you how as I wrap up this book with my own experiences.

9.2 He is the Joy Giver

Habakkuk 3:17-19 [KJV]

[17]*Although the fig tree shall not blossom, neither shall fruit be in the vines, the labour of the olive shall fail, and the fields shall yield no meat.*

[18]*yet I will rejoice in the LORD, I will joy in the God of my salvation.*

¹⁹ The LORD is my strength; he will make my feet like hind's feet, and He will make me o walk upon mine high places.

If you take a critical look at the scriptures above, you will realise that conditions abound that are possible joy killers.

What can be worse than living from hand to mouth? Every source of livelihood has gone and one is left empty and almost a beggar? Look at the next verse, the writer has it established in his heart that nothing has the power to take his joy from him because he has received it from The Source Himself.

He says that the Joy of Salvation or faith in God's salvation is his reason for constant joy and thanksgiving.

This is the attitude we must put up, no matter what temporary situation we find ourselves in. The truth is that God, through The Holy Ghost takes over the situation and helps us sail through the season.

The knowledge of our salvation sets us free from the past, gives us faith for the present and a glorious hope for the future. Hope for the future gives joy and faith for the present gives peace.

It was through this type of situation that I had the vision to write this book 'Pathways to unlimited Joy'. It is important to state that a Christian can live a joyful life regardless of what they are going through.

When I reflect on all that I have been through in my life, I see a lot. During the process, if you had told me that there was anything called 'Unlimited joy', I would have said 'No, I doubt it'. Now I have come to realize that we can indeed have unlimited joy through the grace of God.

Now, I have a story about my life's journey. From being a person that could hear to someone that is categorised with hearing impediment - the category of people that cannot hear well or have acquired deafness (mine is the acquired one).

It has been twenty years or thereabouts. This happened to me as an adult. That was a time of my life that left me devastated. You can imagine how devastated I was, to say the least. I was not just stressed; I was also distressed. I was anxious about my future as well.

I wondered how I would continue living from that point, manage my relationships with people, and continue with my job and whether I would need to learn special communication skills.

I was worried about everything I thought could happen to a person that loses any of their senses. All these overwhelmed me at some point, but I did not remain at that phase without the help of God. He picked me up and gave me a special hearing ability – the ability to hear His voice and take instructions that will help others in the same situation. As they come across this book, they will be strengthened and given hope.

My purpose now is to tell this story to empower others and enable them to see light at the end of their tunnels. Regardless of what they are going through right now, they too can have unlimited Joy like I am enjoying.

It brings satisfaction hat through the grace and favour of God this book will add value and joy to people's lives.

The Joy of serving my generation and generations to come keeps me going, no matter what. My purpose is to serve the world with joy. I am on assignment to be used of the Lord as an oil of joy to humanity.

I am a wife, mother, civil servant and Pastor. I also run a business and I am an author of five books and counting. I have a lot of things going on, however as I mentioned earlier, the journey of my deafness would have prevented me from actually doing anything because it was a hidden disability. Unless I tell you or spend some time with you, you will not detect it.

This particularly put me in so many difficult situations where people misjudged and misunderstood me. We all know that answering the telephone is an important part of any job, business, ministry and doing so became very difficult and impossible for me.

It got to a time when all those were severely affected so much so that I became confused. Imagine picking up a phone and being unable to hear the dialling tone or you just think you are dialling a number that is not working or that there is no connection because you cannot hear anything. That was the beginning of my confusion. Imagine the light indicator of your phone is flashing to inform you that you have a call but when you pick up, you put down the phone because you think no one is there, that was my story. My phone vibrates where I sit but I will not know that I am actually missing a call. Imagine somebody afar of, hearing the phone. I have tried to remember when traffic became silent and sound in general became less intrusive.

Though the pace of life is fast, busy and hectic at times, the sound I heard did not reflect all the hustle and bustle of times. It seemed like people were suddenly talking softly or mumbling. What a conundrum! I will pause and look to see if there was anything happening around. I see people. Imagine asking people to repeat themselves "sorry, can you say that again?" This became a constant part of my statements and conversations. It was always "Madam, I am sorry. I did not catch what you said", "sorry, I missed what you said", "sorry, I don't understand what you are saying, can you speak louder please", "can you speak a little slower please?", Then the person's look will say "is she alright?" or "what is her problem?" or in some cases, "whatever".

This led me to what I can call, depression, because at that time, I was not sure about what was wrong with me. What about the time that people misheard me or when I made a statement and they took it a different way because of my pronunciation. I did not know anymore because I could not even hear myself properly and therefore my communication also was affected. Imagine that you have to lip read and try to look at people directly on their faces before you can put together what they were saying. I would hear certain things like 'Utter' instead of 'outer'. That was my story.

I remember one day, when I was on a train to London and I did not hear the announcement, I was left on the train by myself until someone came to tell me that that was the end of the trip. "Oh, I am sorry" was my response. It was just series of confusion upon confusion and embarrassment upon embarrassment.

I think it was at that point that I told myself not again. I had to talk to myself. I became aware that indeed something is wrong. Why was I not interacting with people like I used to? I knew something was different, was it me or them? I was not sure.

I decided to go to the hospital for a hearing test, but my general practitioner {GP} referred me to the Audiology department in Ear, Eyes, Nose and Throat hospital. While waiting for the appointment, I became anxious, depressed and sometimes destructive. I did not want to think that I am deaf or had become deaf, but I acknowledged that there was a possibility.

When I got the appointment at last, I went to the hospital and the hearing test was conducted, it revealed that I was indeed losing my hearing.

At this point, I would like to say that it has been a journey indeed but God helped me and continues to lead me through with unlimited Joy. I strongly believe the bible verse that says that the Lord is my strength and I know he will continue to be my strength.

The diagnosis of my hearing was not a news that I took lightly and I do not think that anyone would, because the test revealed that I was losing my hearing enough to be considered deaf or hearing impaired.

When the test result was announced and given to me I was in denial. I said "No, way, I cannot believe it". A part of me thought that I had definitely misheard. My shock was too much to comprehend the diagnosis. What? Not me. When? How did it happen? Why me? Maybe you thought this or you may have exclaimed it as well. My own decision was that I will not accept it. I am not disabled - this was the thought that was racing through my mind. I compared myself with others that I have seen living with this disability, both in real life and movies, it was just unbelievable and unacceptable by me.

Have you been there? In a phase where you lived in denial? I lived in a state of denial for two whole years.

It was then that life became more difficult, more miserable that even in my fellowship, no one understood what I was going through. I was really suffering in silence. It affected me totally as well as my confidence and self-esteem. I could not face anyone to tell them what I was going through because the few people I told misjudged me. They said I needed to confess my sin if I had sinned and this brings to mind that why people judge others passing through life's challenge just from their own perspective. They look at others with their hypocritical lenses, diagnosing the problem from a very high sanctimonious or religious seat that God has not placed them on.

I was misjudged and because I wanted a solution and my self-esteem had reduced. I unconsciously accepted their judgement as I began to search myself, to see if I had committed any sin. I went to my closet and said, "Lord, if I had committed sin, I am sorry, forgive me, have mercy on me". After praying seriously and moving from one prayer meeting to another, I could not just comprehend what I had done to lose my hearing. At this point, my faith was going up and down, it was only the Joy of the Lord that kept me or better put, it was the Grace of God.

I remembered the story of Apostle Paul when he was in a dire situation and went to God. God replied him and said His grace was sufficient for him. I knew I had to cling unto God asking for his grace to be sufficient because it was getting to a point where I was losing my mind. I was so stressed out and constantly tearful that it was affecting my job.

At some point I was referred to take assessments at the hospital and the result was still that I was losing my hearing.

In the heat of all these, my employer was not willing to take any explanations, rather, they expected me to perform as usual. That also affected my confidence. I could not attend meetings or take minutes of meetings anymore. It was a difficult journey and life of isolation, so to speak. I found it difficult to tell others that I could not hear well, however, I continued trusting God. I remember that at some point, I said to him that I would do anything for Him if he just healed me of my hearing loss. The answer came, even though it was not exactly as I asked but I still have joy.

It has been years now and over these years, I am still praying and trusting God but the Joy of the Lord has been my strength. I know I said to God that if He can see me through, I will write books to glorify His name and tell others about his faithfulness. I will encourage others and this is part of what I am doing with this book.

His word says, *'When thou passeth through the waters, I will be with thee, and through the rivers, they shall not overflow thee. When thou walkest through the fire, thou shallt not be burned, neither shall the flame kindle upon thee'* Isaiah 43:2 [KJV].

He also says, *'There hath no temptation taken you but such as is common to man; but God is faithful, who will not suffer you to be tempted that ye are able, but will with the temptation also make a way to escape, that ye may be able to bear it'* 1 Corinthians 10:13 [KJV].

My book titled 'Exchanging my disability for God's ability' has additional details about this. You can check my website for my books, see under contact details.

When we compare ourselves with others, we are actually robbing ourselves of our joy and we will not have that joy which is our strength because we will always see ourselves as small and unable to achieve our goals. When we see ourselves in the light of God, we become stronger and more fulfilled.

Pain as a Business Woman

I have done several businesses and lost money in the past but the major one that threw me off balance was when I borrowed money for an investment and within 24 hours, I was conned into investing the money in a wrong business. Guess what, I lost the money. How do I find joy in this situation? I have heard about people being duped and cheated out of their possessions and I used to wonder how such could happen. However, when I experienced it, I realised that anyone could be a victim.

The journey was difficult. 'Oh, no!' That was how I reacted when I realised that I have been conned and duped. I screamed my head off when I realised that the loan I took from the bank to do a business ended up in a wrong investment. I screamed and lamented. I was almost going crazy realizing that there was no way I could get the money back. For days, I was not myself as I thought life was no longer worth living. I concluded that there was no hope for me. I was devastated and looked so stupid. I could not believe myself.

I shared this particular story to encourage someone that has probably been a victim of fraud or shocking business losses that took him or her back to ground zero. You must realise that it could have been worse because there is no loss that is as bad as loss of life.

The Bible in Ecclesiastes 9:4 [KJV] says, 'For to him who is joined to all the living there is hope, for a living dog is better than a dead lion'.

I want to encourage such person to know that where there is life, there is always hope. This is what kept me through it all and is still keeping me.

Don Moen in one of his famous songs said 'God will make a way where there seems to be no way, He works in ways we cannot see, He will make a way for me, He will be my guide hold me closely to His side. With love and strength for each new day, He will make a way, He will make a way'.

Have you been in that situation where you ask yourself "what happened"? I was there and it was not an easy journey, I was disappointed at myself as well as the person involved. I was disappointed about the fact that

I did not do my due diligence before investing money in such a business, but through it all, God has been my strength.

I had to accept what happened and moved on because it started affecting my health, my job and my relationship with the people I loved. On the periphery one would wonder how would I find joy in this situation, but I was able to encourage myself as David did. I encouraged myself in the Lord that I can make it again.

With God on my side, I am no longer where I used to be, I can see a bright future.

Regardless of what you are going through or the type of losses that you have encountered, take heart because you will come out triumphant.

A Great man of God once said, 'put me in a desert, I will produce again'. This was because he knew the God he serves. It is not about you, the circumstance, or the event. It is about the God you serve. He created you for His pleasure which means he delights in your prosperity, so why should He allow you wallow in pain?

Delight yourself in Him and watch Him take over. I am a testimony of this awesome power. Right now, without contradictions I can encourage you through this medium and let you know that you can make it again. It is not over until God says so.

He is The God of the twenty-four hour miracle. Just like the rod of Aaron budded overnight and shocked the Elders in Israel who wanted to undermine his call, you too can rise again. Your business, your health and anything that the enemy has stolen can be restored in Jesus name.

Do not let your hope die because I have kept mine alive. Square shoulders because soon you shall testify.

DOXOLOGY

You have read my story and seen the Hand of God clearly written all over. I take no credit for how things turned out or who I am today. All credit goes to Him who holds all the power, the world and they that are in it, in His Hands.

This book will not be complete if I do not give you the opportunity to enjoy the privilege of knowing and having Him as a Father. So, if you have not had an encounter with this Jesus, I will like you to say this prayer. Perhaps you received him but lost the relationship. Please rededicate your life to Him and I can assure you that you too will one day tell the world about this JOY.

Dear Father God, I come before you, recognising and accepting that I am a sinner.

I ask that Jesus, who died on the cross for me and rose from the dead, washes me by the blood and comes into my heart. I renounce my past and receive your life now. Give me that joy that no one can give.

Thank You for the new life. In Jesus name I pray, Amen.

If you said all this prayer with all your heart and without any doubt, then you are already a child of God. All that a Christian ought to enjoy, is now yours to enjoy too.

All you need to do is to get a Bible and begin to study and fellowship in a Bible believing Church because you need to grow in Him. The Holy Spirit who is the Greatest Teacher will help you.

God bless you, Shalom.

Contacts:

To contact the author, purchase her other great books

or to enrol on our online course: Joyful Living Program.

Exchanging My Disability for God's Ability

A Child's Guide to Prayer

A Prayer Guide for Parents and Grandparents

or to enrol on our online course: Joyful Living Program.

Please visit: www.joyofmanygenerations.com

Email: info@joyofmanygenerations.com

Printed in Great Britain
by Amazon

85954829R00058